# INTERIOR COLOR BY DESIGN

## *A design tool for architects, interior designers, and facility managers*

### COMMERCIAL EDITION

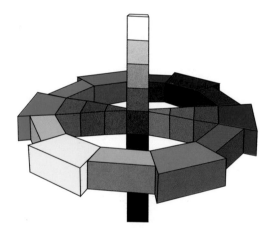

**SANDRA L. RAGAN, FIBD**

ROCKPORT
PUBLISHERS

**ROCKPORT PUBLISHERS**
**ROCKPORT, MASSACHUSETTS**

*To my Mother, who reminded*
*me I used to color on the walls!*

Book design and production by
Sara Day Graphic Design
Illustrations by Jonathan Poore

Copyright © 1995 by
Rockport Publishers, Inc.

First published in the United States of America by:
Rockport Publishers, Inc.
146 Granite Street
Rockport, Massachusetts 01966
Telephone: (508) 546-9590
Fax: (508) 546-7141
Telex: 5106019284 ROCKORT PUB

Other Distribution by:
Rockport Publishers, Inc.
Rockport, Massachusetts 01966

ISBN 1-56496-119-2

1  3  5  7  9  10  8  6  4  2

Printed in Hong Kong

# CONTENTS

# INTRODUCTION

True design talent is being able to visualize a finished interior during the design process. The best interior designs harmonize form, space, light, texture, and color. Of all of these aspects, color is the integral element in every design. Predicting and controlling nuances of color to achieve the desired result is an intuitive process, but a greater understanding of color allows even the most successful interior designers and architects to be responsive to client goals and needs.

*Interior Color By Design: Commercial Edition* is a design tool for architects, interior designers, and facility managers who make color choices for commercial environments. Whether it is used as a primer or refresher on the world of color, this book will broaden your understanding of how color works and how it can work for you. It is specifically designed to let you visually experiment with and design color schemes.

Part I covers basic color theory and its application in commercial spaces. Richly colored interiors demonstrate the principles of color theory and the effects that color has on the commercial environment. Part II is a compilation of sample color combinations designed to work as a library of color ideas. Sample interiors illustrate each of the color schemes (discussed in Chapter 2) and color chips that show variations on each color scheme follow each interior.

In commercial spaces, color has a tremendous effect on the occupants and users of the space: proper color choices can make an office more productive, a retail space more profitable, a nursing home more pleasant, and a doctor's office more comfortable. Once you understand color theory, you can allow your intuition to take over, and even break the rules to fit the situation. Color can energize, soothe, cool, or warm when used in the right combinations in the right locations. It can help to focus workers, unify a large corporation, create the ambiance for a nightclub or a restaurant, or draw people into a retail store. *Interior Color By Design: Commercial Edition* presents fundamental interior design principles, techniques, and examples that will contribute to the successful interior design of commercial environments.

Photo: Paul Warchol

5

PART I

## ATTRIBUTES

Every color is defined by three major attributes: hue, value, and chroma. These are considered the dimensions of a color. Understanding these dimensions and their relationship to one another will help you to fully understand color. To fully describe any color, it is necessary to first define all three of these attributes.

### HUE AND THE COLOR WHEEL

The first attribute of color is its name, or hue, such as purple, red, or blue. Color is best understood by reference to the color wheel, which represents the basic hues, or colors, of the spec-

trum. There are an infinite number of colors and grades of color but, for simplicity, the most common color wheel is made up of 12 colors, all at their full intensity.

### VALUE

The relative lightness or darkness of a color—its *value*—is the second attribute of color. Value of a color is achieved by adding white to lighten a color, or adding black to darken a color. Colors with white added are called *tints*, and colors with black added are called *shades*. A test to determine colors of equal value is to take a black and white photo of the space. The equal values will appear as the same gray in the photo.

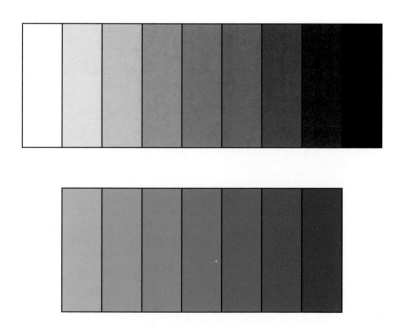

*Fig. 1.1* Color wheel

*Fig. 1.2* Gray value scale and red value scale

CHROMA

The third attribute of color is *chroma*, or saturation. This is the intensity, or essence, of color; chroma is determined by the amount of gray added to it. On a chroma scale, only the intensity of a color varies, not its value.

**Fig. 1.3** *Red chroma scale*

**A color + black = shade**
**A color + white = tint or pastel**
**A color + gray = tone**

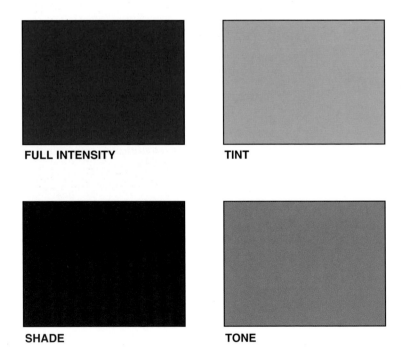

FULL INTENSITY      TINT

SHADE      TONE

**Fig. 1.4** *Tint, shade, and tone of red*

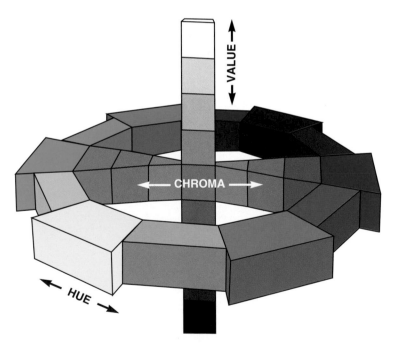

**Fig. 1.5** *Hue, value, and chroma—the three dimensions of color*

## TEMPERATURE

Light, color, and temperature are all interrelated. Light radiates heat; the more light, the more heat. Therefore, colors are referred to as "warm" colors or "cool" colors. Red, orange, and yellow are on the warm side of the spectrum, and blue, green, and violet are the coolest colors. Red is the hottest color, while blue is the coolest. There are also degrees of warmth or coolness of colors, such as cooler shades of red and warmer shades of blue. This is determined by the proportion of the hues mixed to achieve the particular shade.

Colors also elicit physiological and psychological responses. Warm colors appear to advance toward the viewer in relationship to other colors, while cool colors recede. Cool colors are naturally soothing, while warm colors excite and arouse.

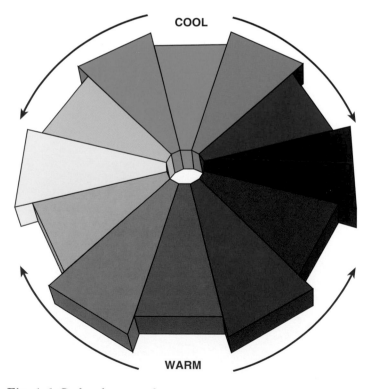

**Fig. 1.6** *Cool and warm colors*

*A warm color scheme sets the emotional tone and stimulates appetites in a posh New York restaurant's private dining room. Notice how coves illuminated with incandescent light enhance the warmth of the space.*

*Colored lights elevate the cold atmosphere of a nightclub and add energy and tension to the environment. Yellow filters on the lights balance the cool color palette.*

## LIGHTING

Natural white light is the presence of all color. Black is the absence of all light and therefore the absence of all color. Colored light mixed together is known as *additive* color. The primary colors of light are red, green, and blue; when combined in equal amounts, they produce white light. A color of lighter value is the result of two colored lights being added together. For example, overlapping green with red light results in yellow light. These additive colors are frequently used in bars, night-clubs, and theaters.

To create dramatic commercial spaces, designers often employ both light and pigment. Combinations of paint pigments behave very differently than combinations of light.

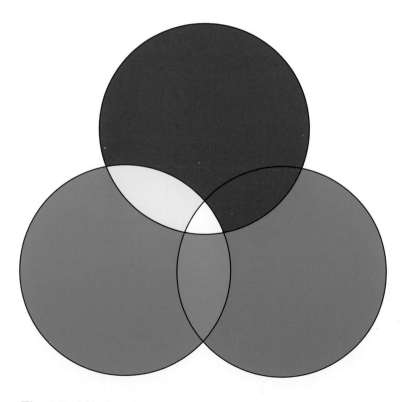

**Fig. 1.7** *Additive color*

*Outside light and a sweeping view were major considerations in this lobby design. Interior finishes and incandecent up-lights enhance the form and shape of the architecture and the changing colors of the skyline. The effective use of neutrals keeps the focus on the exterior.*

*Fully saturated colors of black, gray, and red are energized by three light sources; natural daylight, incandescent light, and fluorescent light. Bold colors work well here; less saturated color would wash out.*

*A seafood restaurant uses cool blue light insets to give the graphic black and white bar an underwater dimension.*

Photo: Max MacKenzie

In addition to colored light, natural light also affects color. Natural northern light has a cold, greenish cast, while a southern light casts a warm pink glow. Eastern light makes color look bleached out, yellowish, and harsh. Western light produces a radiant red-orange color effect.

Designers must consider all light sources that will affect the environment they are creating. For example, fluorescent light gives color a bluish cast unless color-corrected bulbs are used. In commercial spaces, the increasingly popular tungsten and halogen lighting gives off very bright yellow and blue casts respectively. Incandescent lighting casts a yellow-orange glow.

Surfaces where the light source color and the pigment color are the same will look gray.

14

Photo: Richard Mandelkorn

# MIX

## SUBTRACTIVE COLOR

It is important to understand the relationship between color and light; additive color is one aspect of this relationship, *subtractive* color is another. Subtractive color is based on the part of the light surfaces reflect back, versus the part of light that is absorbed.

Red, yellow, and blue are the primary subtractive colors. All other colors are a derivative of these three. Primary colors are at equal distance from one another on the color wheel. Mixing two primary colors together creates each of the secondary colors—

orange, purple, and green. Secondary colors are located between the primary colors on the color wheel. When a primary color and its adjacent secondary color are mixed together they create *tertiary* color. The tertiary colors are yellow-green, green-blue, blue-violet, red-orange, yellow-orange, and yellow-green.

To keep colors clear, use pure hues without black or white added to them. For strong tones, use a single color with a proportion of black added to it. Mixing two or more colors with black added to them results in dull, muted hues. The same is true of tints; use only one color with white added to it, then add clear colors to acheive the desired hue.

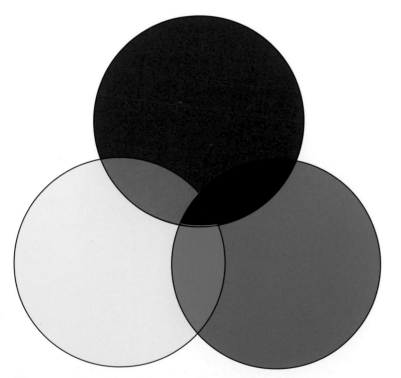

*Fig. 1.8* Subtractive colors

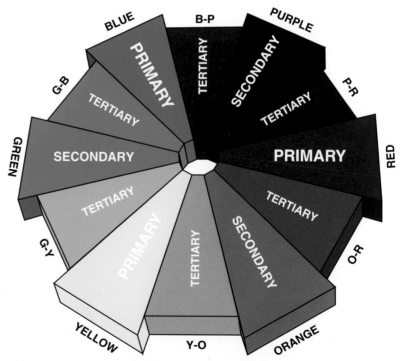

*Fig. 1.9* Color wheel with primaries, secondaries, and tertiaries labeled

The large expanse of cool color on the floor balances the warm colors to create visual harmony in this showroom space. The most visually interesting spaces use both warm and cool colors.

Warm light envelops the highly textured surfaces of this restaurant. Discordant colors on the chairs break all the rules, but work to create a dynamic, happy atmosphere.

16

Photo: Paul Warchol

*In this space, the primary colors of red, yellow, and blue demonstrate color hierarchy. Although the three colors are used in equal proportions, the red appears to advance the most, followed by the yellow and then the blue. Red actually elicits a physiological response; the viewer's eye sees it as visually closer.*

PARTITIVE COLOR

Granite, when viewed from a distance, looks gray, but up close it is really two distinct colors—black and white. Blending or mixing colors together while keeping one color distinct allows the designer to create the illusion of a third color. This process is known as *partitive* color. Glazing walls with different colors to achieve a third, or stippling a finish, are techniques which incorporate both the use of texture and partitive color. Partitive color can also create subtle tones and multicolored effects. Use partitive color, as well as a variety of textures, to define and bring depth to the space.

## TEXTURE

The perception of color rests with the eye of the observer. It is also affected by the quality of light, the texture of the finish (flat, matte, or gloss,) and the surface of the material.

Textures change the appearance of color. When a surface is rough, color looks darker than the same shade applied to a smooth surface. This is due to the shadows the rough finish creates. A very fine, smooth surface reflects more light and causes the color applied to it to appear lighter. Color applied to matte or dull surfaces will always look darker than color on a very slick, finished surface. Be aware that slick surfaces and dark colors will show every imperfection if the surface is not perfect.

*The curved wall demonstrates the properties of partitive color; one color next to another creates the illusion of a third.*

*Texture, color, and light all play an important role in the design of this entrance lobby. The contrast of slick, black marble tile and warm, painted wood gives the surfaces a rich feeling. A blue-painted reveal in the ceiling adds drama. This is a good example of the temperature and color of natural materials.*

*Overlaying color gives the walls of a restaurant soft, deep texture, and brings warmth to the shadowed corners.*

19

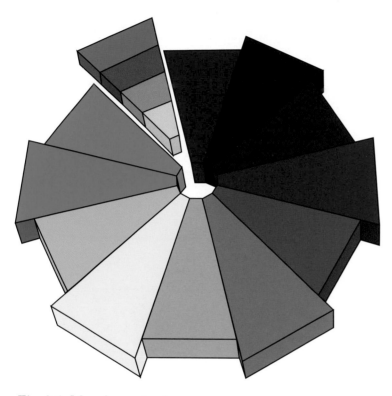

**Fig. 2.1** *Monochromatic colors*

## MONOCHROMATIC

A monochromatic color palette uses only one color and values of that color to create depth and interest. The most common monochromatic color scheme employs white, black, and gray. These schemes are dramatic, very sophisticated, and sometimes elegant. They rely on the user's ability to see subtle differences between shades. Monochromatic schemes are often used in law offices, private hotel suites, and upscale retail stores.

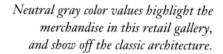

*Neutral gray color values highlight the merchandise in this retail gallery, and show off the classic architecture.*

Photo: Bruce Katz

*The black, white, and gray scheme on the facing page shifts dramatically from one end of the value scale to the other. Large shifts in values make a bold statement that is particularly suitable for contemporary interiors.*

## ANALOGOUS

Analogous color schemes use three colors—or their tints and shades—that are next to each other on the color wheel. Analogous color schemes can be cool or warm color combinations—such as blue, blue-violet, and violet, or red, red-orange, and orange. These schemes are filled with energy and are good design choices for lively places like sports facilities, day-care centers, schools, and health clubs.

Analogous schemes can mix warm and cool colors, creating energetic schemes like red-violet, red, and red-orange, or schemes as soothing as tropical waters, such as blue-green, green, and yellow-green.

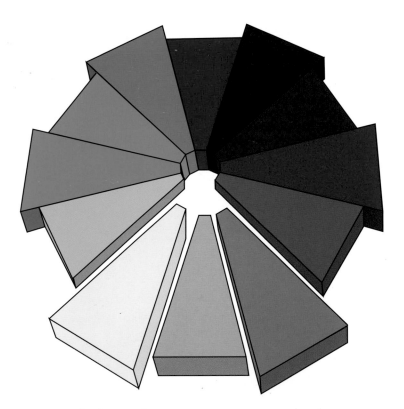

**Fig. 2.2** *Analogous colors*

*A fresco dictates the color scheme in this Italian restaurant. Color proportion and intuition all played strong roles in creating this analogous scheme.*

22

Photo: Paul Warchol

*Subdued shades of yellow-green, yellow, and orange create a harmonious yet energetic scheme for this office.*

Photo: Paul Warchol

Photo: Nick Merrick / Herman Miller, Inc.

*Bold analogous colors define the floor planes in this multi-story building. Notice how the use of color develops the vertical rhythm of the architecture.*

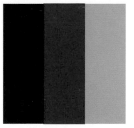

*Red accents balance a cool color scheme and keep an office design temperate.*

23

## NEUTRAL

More interesting than the monochromatic color palette, neutral color schemes contain deeper values of colors, such as off-white, neutral gray, beige, tan, and light taupe. These schemes are neither warm nor cool and are considered refined, formal, and elegant.

Neutrals build upon color value. Contrasting neutral schemes placed next to one another gain strength. They are often used in financial institutions, upscale restaurants, hotels, and places that want a soft but formal atmosphere. A neutral scheme can be used as a background for a single strong accent color, or for a fine collection of art.

*Warm wood tones accent this neutral room and bring a restful cozy atmosphere to a private hospital room.*

*The understatement of a neutral color scheme can lend strength to a design, as it does in this sophisticated conference room.*

*Neutral color schemes make an ideal background for art. Here a lobby in multi-shades of taupe offers a formal welcome.*

## COMPLEMENTARY

Complementary color palettes are colors from opposite sides of the color wheel. These are the boldest, most contrasting hues. They can also be the most difficult to properly balance. Complements are harmonious. Look at the examples and study the nuances of good complementary schemes. Retail stores, shopping malls, and wholesale stores often use complementary schemes to create an energetic atmosphere. These schemes are used to energize spaces, for they are cheerful and lively. They may also be found in the offices of advertising agencies, brokers, and real estate agents.

Photo: Paul Warchol

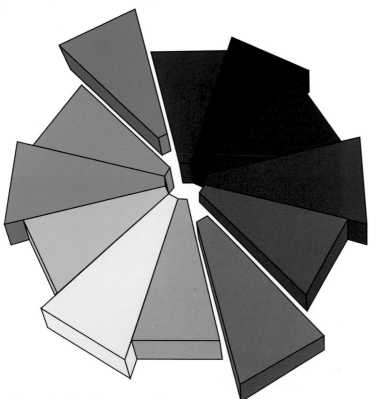

**Fig. 2.3** *Complementary colors*

*The golden wood of a serpentine desk complements purple carpet in this receiving area. Throughout the office complementary colors are echoed by complementary rough and smooth textures.*

*Orange carpet in combination with blue conference chairs presents a complementary color scheme at its best. The painting neatly mirrors the shapes, colors, and design of the room.*

*Complements of deep green and red are inviting, but close enough in value to keep the atmosphere composed.*

27

## SPLIT COMPLEMENT

More complex than the complementary color scheme, a split complement palette makes use of one hue on one side of the color wheel and the two hues adjacent to its complement color. Purple with yellow-green and yellow-orange is an example of a split complement scheme. The two adjacent colors are harmonious, while the complement adds the vibrant contrast. Since split complement schemes express action and activity, use them to create impact and when there are many surfaces to consider.

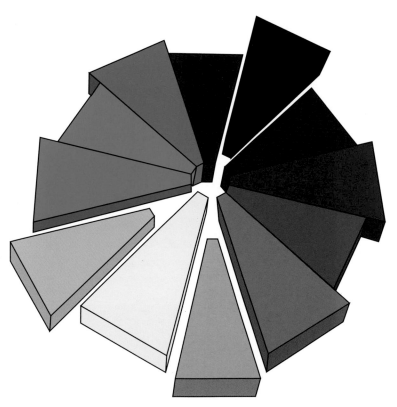

**Fig. 2.4** *Split complements*

*The use of multiple bright, clear hues creates colorful excitement in this child care facility.*

Photo: Ron Blunt

In this contemporary restaurant, a split complement color scheme gains its balance from the cherry red tone of a wooden column. A golden band of color above the exposed beams gives the ceiling visual height and adds its warm glow to a pleasant atmosphere for dining.

Here the a split complement scheme of primary colors enlivens gray-hammered walls and makes a statement of power, energy, and fun.

29

## TRIAD

The triad color scheme uses any three colors spaced equally around the color wheel. The most typical triad scheme is that of the primaries—red, blue, and yellow. In this scheme, you can immediately see the color hierarchy. These schemes tend to be bold and showy and are best used for large spaces such as schools, sports arenas, and movie theaters. However, if you vary the value of the color, you can create a more sophisticated contrast.

Look at the triad schemes presented here, and carefully study the value of the colors and their spacing on the wheel. Maintaining the same spacing, rotate around the color wheel for other successful triad color combinations.

Photo: Richard Mandelkorn

*In this triad scheme, the red brick ceiling tile and teal painted doorframes balance visually stimulating yellow walls. The balance of color allows the reception space to be bold without seeming garish.*

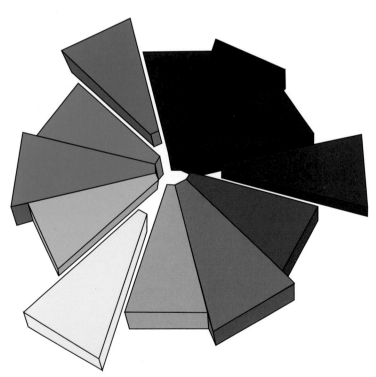

**Fig. 2.5** *Triads*

30

*Primary colors portray a whimsical atmosphere in this office reception area. Notice how the fully saturated red of the corridor wall moves toward the reception area.*

Photo: Alan Weintraub

*Triad colors of pink, blue, and yellow elicit a strong response from clients in this computer demonstration area. Varying the value of red gives a common palette new interest.*

The placement of color in commercial environments plays a major role in creating the mood of the space. In fact, color strongly affects the way an environment is perceived by its occupants. Through impression or association, color has a psychological impact. The colors chosen for a design scheme change the comfort or success of a space—whether it is a commercial office, hospital, retail store, bank, or government facility.

Color contributes to the productivity and to the psychological satisfaction of the occupants in a space. Use the following examples to explore the role color plays in creating just the right commercial environment.

## OFFICES

Today, office environments must meet many needs. Flexible office spaces accommodate employees whose tasks range from traditional office work to worldwide teleconferencing. Each area of the office should be considered as an independent element, as well as part of the whole. In the design process, the image the client wants to project and the functions that will occur in the space dictate the design requirements. The same considerations apply to the selection of color for an office; aesthetics, surfaces, the volume of the space, the psychological effects of particular colors, and context should all be taken into account. Good aesthetics are especially important, as they can contribute to job satisfaction as well as to increased productivity.

When selecting colors for the commercial environment, carefully consider their reflectance values. Light reflectance refers to the amount of light a surface reflects. The higher the reflectance, the brighter the space; the lower the reflectance, the darker the space. White reflects 80 percent of the light it receives, black reflects 5 percent. Interior offices with no windows should have colors with a reflectance value of 65 to 70 percent, to compensate for the lack of natural light. Perimeter offices with windows and computer environments should have colors with about 50 percent reflectance.

*Photo: Paul Warchol*

*The full chroma blue wall focuses attention and heightens the illusion of depth. A black and white marble floor, and black reception desk sharpen the richness of bold color.*

*On the facing page, the combination of deep wood tones and warm golden walls suggests stability and security in this office space. The ceiling, walls, and floor are all of similar values; the deeper values and texture of the columns highlights restored architecture.*

33

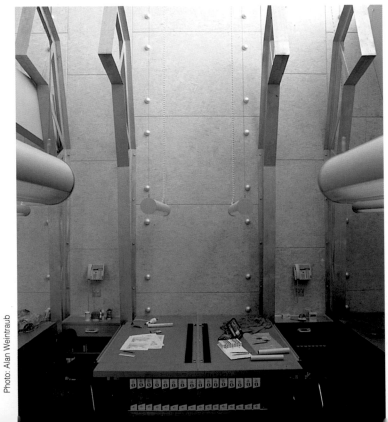

*Blue carpeting creates a substantial base for the gray neutral palette of a design studio. Although gray can be shadowy, here it is the right choice—the neutral background focuses attention on the design work, and does not conflict with the project at hand.*

*Dominant colors on the floor, walls, and ceiling define the tonality of this space. Chairs and dividers in complementary shades bring harmony to the work environment.*

## COLOR AND LOCATION

*Where color is used in an office environment is also important. A blue wall can define space, a green floor can appear relaxing, a gray ceiling may appear illusive and shadowy. People respond both psychologically and physiologically to color, form, and texture. Successful design is built on the success of the color scheme; it must be attractive and conducive to the tasks performed in the space.*

34

*A triad scheme enfolds an uncluttered reception room in rich color. Warm, creamy wall color balances the grayed plum accents in the painting and rug; cooler blue-green tones throughout the space inspire concentration. Lighter, clearer colors are growing in importance in interior design*

*Saturated color is used as an organizing element in this corporate headquarters. Different colors of core wall define each area, and give work environments on each floor a different ambience.*

36

*Neutral colors and texture are woven into a sophisticated backdrop for this collection of art and artifacts.*

*Red, the most dynamic of all colors, grabs attention in this private office. This office says power; the color choices reflect a confident energetic corporate leader.*

37

*Geometric shapes and planes of high value hues play with each other in an otherwise white office space. The crisp contrast between white and a partial rainbow of color makes a very complex scheme; the discordant colors are surprising and wonderful.*

*Monochromatic schemes of lighter values make good color solutions for difficult areas. In this conference room the scheme serves as a beautiful backdrop to the art and focuses attention on the skyline.*

## CARE ENVIRONMENTS

In care environments color contributes to the psychological and physiological well-being of the users of the space. Hospitals, doctors' offices, clinics, children's day-care centers, continuing life facilities, and nursing homes are all care facilities. The designer's choice of color for a hospital or a regular clinic interior influences how visitors feel in the space. Green was once used in all medical offices, because it is a healing and tranquil color. Color experts have come to realize that stimulation in care environments is also good, so a multitude of colors—warm, arousing shades, and soothing, cool, shades— are now being used.

Neutral colors accented with blue have a physiological effect that lowers blood pressure. Purple in lighter values and yellows in soft shades can actually assist in the healing process. Blue-greens to teals are used in all care environments, from hospitals to continuing care facilities because they bring comfort, calm, and security to a space. Children's areas in hospitals and day-care centers use balanced colors from both the warm and cool spectrum, to calm yet provide visual interest at the same time. Color in care environments should be used to define the space, set the mood, and create a healing atmosphere.

*Clinical care requires a welcoming environment. Here a cool color palette of purple, blue, and green soothes patients waiting for treatment. The warmth of incandescent light keeps the space from being cold and unfriendly.*

Photo: © Tom Crane

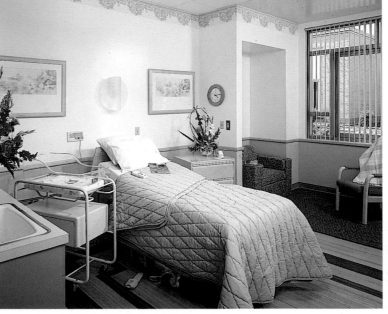

## COLOR AND WELL-BEING

*The analogous color scheme for this surgical center (above) communicates confidence to those entering. The quiet interplay of light and color adds serenity to these surroundings.*

*Warm and cool colors balance each other in this day-care center (top right). Used as accents, fully saturated primary and secondary colors create happy and stimulating surroundings for children.*

*Shades and tints of analogous colors and the warmth of natural wood finishes soften the image of a hospital room (bottom right).*

Harvard Community
Health Plan

*Burlington Center*

Laboratory/Radiology

EXIT

*Zones of stimulating color against soothing neutral backgrounds define waiting and reception areas in this
community health care center. Balanced schemes like this one work well in care environments.*

41

*Vivid color schemes work like a kaleido-
scope; they can be dazzling or disorienting.
Combinations of brilliant colors succeed
when the shapes and patterns in the room
are kept bold and simple.*

*The location of color in a space influences our
reaction to it. In this pediatric waiting room,
blue is used on the floor as a sound base, with
cheerful red and yellow accent colors. If the
same amount of blue had been used on the
walls, it would be overpowering. The familiar
primary colors also help allay children's fears.*

## RETAIL

In retail spaces, color can be used as a tool, to enhance products and displays, entice customers, and establish a store or product's identity.

Understanding the dominance, hierarchy, and proportion of color, and then using colors to enhance products is the key to successful retail design. Very intense, fully saturated colors are often used in retail stores. For example, red and yellow respectively are the most eye-catching colors. Since red appears to advance, the viewer automatically pays attention to it. Used in moderation in displays, red and yellow colors enhance products. Retailers also use color and light together to market their products. Since color plays such an important role in product image, it is especially important to examine colors under the same lighting that will be used in the retail space.

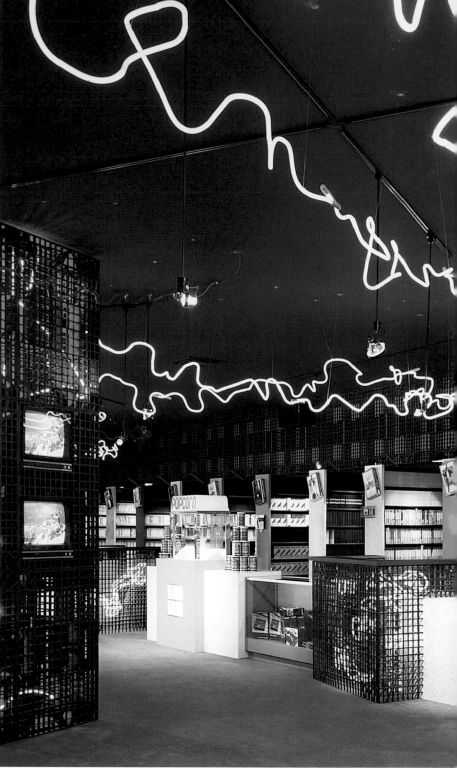

*Deep blue surfaces recede and then literally surround you as you enter this video store. Effective display lighting highlights the merchandise, while neon accent lighting creates the high level of activity you feel in the store.*

Photo: Russell Abraham

43

Photo: Max MacKenzie

## COLOR AND MOTIVATION

*Blue and white accented with black forms a scheme that is cool and modern. The geometric form of a corrugated silver display modulates the space and focuses attention on the merchandise.*

*Graded color hues add depth to a celestial blue-painted sky. The blue ceiling recedes from broken, creamy walls, giving the store an airy atmosphere.*

44

*Muted, rustic colors  make the merchandise stand out in a converted city loft. Aging red brick and worn wooden floors draw attention to the stamped metal counters.*

*A yellow back wall radiates energy, and attracts shoppers into this retail space. Bright color dispersed throughout the store helps repeating rows of racks avoid monotony.*

*The subdued effect of purple is brought to life by red and yellow accents. Notice how the black figure sharpens the yellow light.*

46

*The blue-violet wall intensifies in contrast with the black mannequin. Truly high style, this dominant color would overpower many spaces, but here it brings energy to the urban scheme of black and white.*

47

## RESTAURANTS AND HOSPITALITY

Clients' goals in hospitality design vary as much as those in other commercial environments. The one overriding mission, however, is to attract people into the space—whether it is a restaurant, cafe, or a large hotel, people must feel invited and welcomed. Restaurants choose color schemes that complement their menu or theme, hotels use color palettes as a unifying element, and restaurant chains use color to establish a visual identity.

Ambiance is the major draw for restaurants, often given more importance than the food, and color is the critical element in establishing a mood and shaping space. Popular taste changes quickly in the hospitality business, and lately a premium has been placed on individuality. Facilities, like the ones shown here, strive to establish their own stylized "look" and rely on colorful design to help them achieve it.

*Color defines the intersecting planes and volumes of this space and gives human scale to a large country club room. Dominant chromas advance, grayed chromas recede; here they work in combination to highlight the architecture and tie together a large space.*

Photo: © Steve Whittaker

48

*Form, function, and color develop a dynamic symmetry here. Brilliant blue creates the illusion of a night sky and makes four walls seem to recede to the horizon. Grayed neutrals give weight to false architectural elements.*

Photo: Richard Mandelkorn

*Golden-colored walls define a large, open space in this restaurant. A deeper tone of color on the booths makes them seem even more private. The repetition of pattern and color adds to the intimate atmosphere.*

49

Photo: Paul Warchol

## COLOR AND IDENTITY

*Large blocks of color layered above the patterned tile wainscot give walls geometric dimension.*

*Warm red ignites a restaurant with stimulating, expansive energy. The industrial black floor and neutral divider contain the color somewhat; red tables and chairs appear like bright blooms of color throughout the room.*

Photo: Russell Abraham

50

*Color contrasts with form in this polished nightclub. Black defines objects and makes colors look crisp; it also anchors the viewer's focus among the many polished surfaces.*

*Orange mellows traditional red in an exotic design for a restaurant. Color defines the architectural features of the space, creating rooms within rooms.*

52

*Simple, pure color in warm tones casts a flattering glow over a small cafe.*

Photo: Barbara Bourne

## PART II

### THE COLOR SAMPLES

Millions of colors are visible to the human eye. The combinations in the pages that follow are intended to educate and inspire your color imagination into creating schemes of your own. The number of combinations and effects that can be achieved are limitless. Your skill and imagination will take you into schemes that you have never before explored. Here we use basic color scheme categories as examples.

For each section, an interior photo is combined with a sample color combination that best reflects the character of the space. Additional color combinations displayed in color chips follow; visually substitute them into the photo to see new color possibilities. With this exercise, you can develop variations on a color scheme or simply use the examples presented. The samples alone form a sourcebook of potential color schemes for ready reference.

55

 **MONOCHROMATIC**

Photo: Donna Kempner

 **MONOCHROMATIC**

 **MONOCHROMATIC**

 **MONOCHROMATIC**

 **MONOCHROMATIC**

 **MONOCHROMATIC**

# MONOCHROMATIC

Photo: Russell Abraham

 **ANALOGOUS**

 **ANALOGOUS**

 **ANALOGOUS**

 **ANALOGOUS**

 **ANALOGOUS**

78

 **ANALOGOUS**

80

 **ANALOGOUS**

 **ANALOGOUS**

**ANALOGOUS**

 **ANALOGOUS**

 **ANALOGOUS**

 **ANALOGOUS**

NEUTRAL

NEUTRAL

Photo: Richard Mandelkorn

**NEUTRAL**

Photo: Richard Mandelkorn

**NEUTRAL**

**NEUTRAL**

**NEUTRAL**

104

**NEUTRAL**

106

**NEUTRAL**

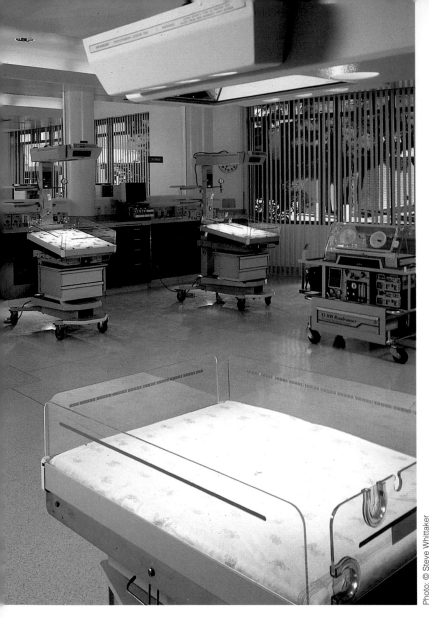

**NEUTRAL**

**NEUTRAL**

**NEUTRAL**

114

 **COMPLEMENTARY**

 **COMPLEMENTARY**

 **COMPLEMENTARY**

120

 **COMPLEMENTARY**

122

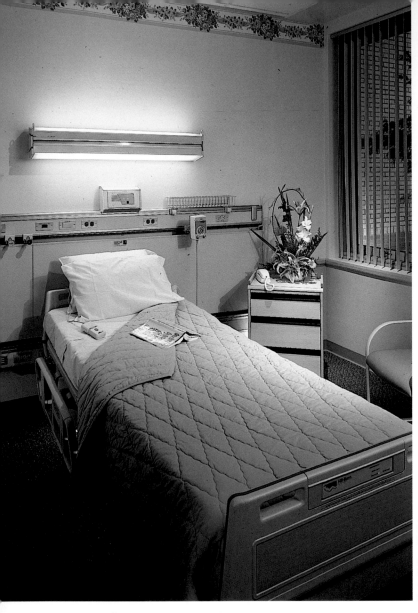

 **COMPLEMENTARY**

 **COMPLEMENTARY**

Photo: © Steve Whittaker

126

Photo: Richard Mandelkorn

 **SPLIT COMPLEMENT**

128

 **SPLIT COMPLEMENT**

130

 **SPLIT COMPLEMENT**

132

 **TRIAD**

 **TRIAD**

Photo: Paul Warchol

 **TRIAD**

138

 **TRIAD**

Photo: Paul Warchol

 **TRIAD**

Photo: Donna Kempner

 **TRIAD**

Photo: Ron Blunt

 **TRIAD**

146

Photo: Paul Warchol

**DISCORDANT**

Photo: Paul Warchol

**DISCORDANT**

150

 **TETRAD**

152

# GLOSSARY

**ADDITIVE COLOR**
Process of mixing colored light. The primary colors of red, green, and blue light make white light when mixed together.

**ANALOGOUS COLORS**
Analogous colors are adjacent to each other on the color wheel.

**CHROMA**
Also referred to as saturation. Chroma is the relative strength or weakness of a color.

**COMPLEMENTARY COLORS**
Colors which are opposite each other on the color wheel, such as red and green.

**COOL COLORS**
Blue-green, blue, and blue-purple are cool colors.

**HUE**
Hue is the name of a color.

**MONOCHROMATIC**
A monochromatic color scheme employs various tints and shades of a single color.

**MONOTONE**
A monotone or neutral color scheme consists of various tints and shades of a neutral color.

**NEUTRAL COLOR**
A color that appears neither warm nor cool, such as gray.

**PARTITIVE COLOR**
Color which is created by mixing many small dots of color which then appear to the eye as a single new color.

**PRIMARY COLORS**
The primary colors of pigments and dyes are red, yellow, and blue. All other colors are derived from these three.

**SATURATION**
Also referred to as chroma, see CHROMA.

**SHADE**
A color created by adding black to a hue.

**SPLIT COMPLEMENTARY COLORS**
Split complementary colors are made up of any color combined with the two colors on either side of its complement.

**SUBTRACTIVE COLOR**
The process of mixing pigments, inks, or dyes. The primary subtractive colors are red, yellow, and blue from which all other colors are derived.

**TETRAD**
A tetrad is any two pairs of complementary colors.

**TINT**
A color created by adding white to a hue.

**TONE**
A color created by adding gray to a hue.

**TONALITY**
The overall impression made by the dominant color in a color scheme.

**TRIAD**
A triad of colors is any three equidistant colors on the color wheel. The primary colors, red, yellow, and blue form a triad.

**VALUE**
The relative lightness or darkness of a color.

**WARM COLOR**
Red, orange, and yellow are warm colors.

Photo: © Steve Whittaker

# BIBLIOGRAPHY

Albers, Josef. Interaction of Color. New Haven CT: Yale University, 1963.

Birren, Faber. Color Psychology and Color Therapy. Secaucus, NJ: University Books, 1961.

Birren, Faber. Light, Color & Environment. Westchester, NY: Schiffer Publishing Ltd., 1988.

Birren, Faber. The Symbolism of Color. New York: Citadel Press, 1988.

Chihiiwa, Hideaki. Color Harmony: A Guide To Creative Color Combinations. Rockport, MA: Rockport Publishers, 1987.

Hope, Augustine and Margaret Walch. The Color Compendium. New York: Van Nostrand Reinhgold, 1990.

Itten, Johannes. Itten: The Elements of Color. New York: Van Nostrand Reinhgold, 1970.

Mahnke, Franke H. and Rudolph H. Mahnke. Color and Light in Man-made Environments. New York: Van Nostrand Reinhgold, 1987.

Sharpe, Deborah T. The Psychology of Color and Design. Chicago: Nelson Hall Company, 1974.

Swirnoff, Lois. Dimensional Color. Boston: Birkhauser Boston, Inc., 1988.

# CREDITS

Cover: © 1994 Paul Warchol
Designer: Quantrell, Mullins & Associates, Inc

p.4 Photographer: Richard Mandelkorn
Designer: Perry Dean Rogers & Partners

p.5 Photographer: Paul Warchol
Designer: Quantrell, Mullins & Associates, Inc

p.6 Photographer: © Steve Whittaker
Designer: Reel Grobeman

p.8 Photographer: Paul Warchol
Designer: Studios Architecture, D.C.

p.11 Photographer: Christopher Little
Designer: Hardy Holzman Pfeiffer Associates

p.12 Photographer: Russell Abraham
Designer: Howard Snoweiss

p.13 Designer: Leo Daly Architects

p.14 (top) Photographer: Max MacKenzie
Designer: Ward-Hale Design Associates, Inc.
Nora Fischer, Michael Finch and Donna Ward-Soloman

p.14 (bottom) Photographer: Richard Mandelkorn
Designer: JCA

p.16 (top) Photographer: Steelcase, Inc.

p.16 (bottom) Photographer: Paul Warchol
Designer: David Rockwell & Jay Haverson formerly of
Haverson Rockwell

p.17 Photographer: Ron Solomon
Designer: Duvall / Hendricks, Inc.

p.18 Photographer: Paul Warchol
Designer: Studios Architecture, D.C.

p.19 (top) Photographer: Paul Warchol
Designer: Quantrell, Mullins & Associates, Inc

p.19 (bottom) Photographer: Richard Mandelkorn
Designer: Ayers Saint Gross Architects

p.20 Photographer: Richard Mandelkorn
Designer: Stein Associates

p.21 Photographer: Bruce Katz
Designer: Alexia N.C.Levite and Brian Levite
The Office of Alexia N.C. Levite

p.22 Photographer: Richard Mandelkorn
Designer: Elkus Manfredi Associates

p.23 (top left) Photographer: Paul Warchol
Designer: Wayne Turett

p.23 (top right) Photographer: Paul Warchol
Designer: Studios Architecture, SFO

p.23 (bottom) Photographer: Nick Merrick / Herman Miller, Inc.

p.24 (left) Photographer: Max MacKenzie
Design: Leo Daly Architects

p.24 (right) Photographer: Richard Mandelkorn

p.25 Photographer: Richard Mandelkorn

p.26 Photographer: Paul Warchol
Designer: Studios Architecture, SFO

p.27 (top) Photographer: Jennie Jones

p.27 (bottom) Photographer: Richard Mandelkorn
Designer: Perry Dean Rogers & Partners

p.28 Photographer: Ron Blunt
Designer: Leo Daly Architects

p.29 (left) Photographer: Richard Mandelkorn
Designer: Stein Associates

p.29 (right) Photographer: Richard Mandelkorn
Designer: Elkus Manfredi Associates

p.30 (top) Photographer: Richard Mandelkorn
Designer: Schwartz Silver Architects

p.30 (bottom) Photographer: Alan Weintraub
Designer: Ace Architects

p.31 Photographer: Paul Warchol
Designer: Studios Architecture, SFO

p.32 Photographer: Jennie Jones

p.33 Photographer: Paul Warchol
Designer: Quantrell, Mullins & Associates, Inc

p.34 (top) Photographer: Steelcase, Inc.

p.34 (bottom) Photographer: Alan Weintraub
Designer: Ace Architects

p.35 Photographer: © Steve Whittaker
Designer: Reel Grobeman

## ACKNOWLEDGMENTS

My gratitude goes to those firms, designers, architects, and photographers who have so graciously contributed their work for inclusion in this book. Without their exceptional talent, this book could not have become a reality. Special thanks to Sue Wood, Cheryl Duvall, Jill Pilaroscia, and Margo Jones for sharing their thoughts on color; to Brenda Edgar for her assistance with the photographic research; to Jonathan Poore for leading the way; and to Rockport Publishers' staff Shawna Mullen, Rosalie Grattaroti, Julie Cleveland, and Barbara States for their continuing support during this endeavor. And most of all, to my husband Tom, for his continuing support of my life goals...

Photo: Paul Warchol

## ABOUT THE AUTHOR

Ms. Sandra Ragan, FIBD, is one of the foremost interior designers in the country, her clients include ITT, AT&T FTS2000, National Geographic, Gallaudet College, Time-Life, Inc. and numerous other associations. She brings to each project a working knowledge of the relationship between environmental psychology and interior design. She is the Past National President of the Institute of Business Designers (IBD), an international organization representing contract interior designers. As a consultant to the National Endowment of the Arts, she has served as an evaluator for OPM's meriting process of interior design for governmental positions.

Ms. Ragan's articles on design in the workplace have appeared in such publications as *The Design Magazine*, *Modern Office Procedures*, *Designer West*, *Regardie's*, and *Contract Magazine*.

Prior to establishing her own studio, Ms. Ragan was part owner and President of Friday Design Group, where for 19 years she led the design team to nationally recognized work. She and her husband, architect Tom Rousselle, maintain design practices in Washington, DC and Biddeford Pool, ME.

Photo: Alan Weintraub